Little Linguists
Learn a Language Book

"AH, SO!"
JAPANESE
FOR KIDS

BY CAROLE MARSH

SAY HON

SAY BOSHI

SAY RINGO

SAY MIDORI

HISTORY · TRIVIA · HUMOR · LANGUAGE and MORE!

EDITOR: CHAD BEARD
COVER DESIGN: VICTORIA DEJOY
GRAPHIC DESIGN & LAYOUT: CECIL ANDERSON AND LYNETTE ROWE

Published by

GALLOPADE™
INTERNATIONAL

800-536-2GET
www.gallopade.com

Gallopade is proud to be a member of these educational organizations and associations:

The National School Supply and Equipment Association (NSSEA)
National Association for Gifted Children (NAGC)
American Booksellers Association (ABA)
Association of Partners for Public Lands (APPL)
Museum Store Association (MSA)
Publishers Marketing Association (PMA)
International Reading Association (IRA)

Carole Marsh Language Books

"HO LEE CHOW!" CHINESE FOR KIDS

"FALSE PAW!" FRENCH FOR KIDS

"AH, SO!" JAPANESE FOR KIDS

"FROM RUSSIA WITH LOVE!" RUSSIAN FOR KIDS

"UH, OH, AMIGO!" SPANISH FOR KIDS

"IT REALLY IS GREEK TO ME!" GREEK FOR KIDS

"SAY WHAT WHEN YOU SNEEZE?!" GERMAN FOR KIDS

"OF ALL THE GAUL!" LATIN FOR KIDS

Math Books

Math for Boys — GRADES 3-6

Math for Girls — GRADES 3-6

Reading and Writing in the Real World!

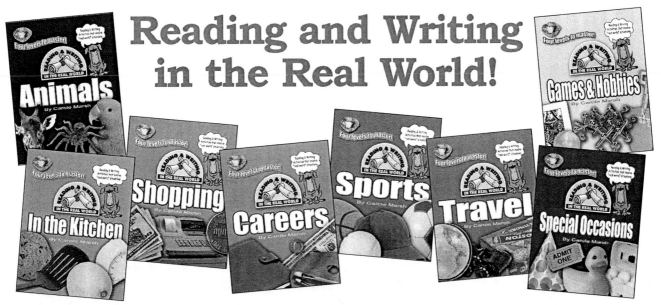

Animals By Carole Marsh

In the Kitchen By Carole Marsh

Shopping By Carole Marsh

Careers By Carole Marsh

Sports By Carole Marsh

Travel By Carole Marsh

Games & Hobbies By Carole Marsh

Special Occasions By Carole Marsh

A WORD FROM THE AUTHOR

One summer, my young son, Michael, and I decided to see if we could learn one language a week OR if we could learn a dozen languages at the same time! That fun adventure resulted in the "Of All the Gaul" language series for kids.

We found that learning any language is fun if you're having fun. We were also surprised to discover how many foreign words we already knew just from our reading in English. In fact, the fact that you often encounter many foreign words and phrases in reading fiction or non-fiction is one reason we wanted to explore a variety of languages.

Michael later said that our summer language study not only helped him with his English (and SAT exam!), but helped him learn which languages he thought he'd like to explore more thoroughly. We both learned it was also more fun when you met another person who spoke a foreign language, and a big help when you traveled to other countries.

Japanese may sound like a very foreign language to you! But, it won't after you read this book!

Carole Marsh

NOTE: This book is an "introduction" to the language. The focus is on why the child should learn some of the language, what the language is, and that they may already know many words in this language. The goal of this book is to get a child excited about the language, familiar with a few of the more common words or phrases they will encounter even in English texts, and eager to take a next more traditional step in learning the language. For languages not in the "ABC" alphabet, the "Romanized" or transliterated version of the language is used.

WHY LEARN JAPANESE ANYWAY?!

Since you already know how to speak one language, why should you bother to learn another? Here are some reasons:

● Because it's very likely that whatever career you end up choosing, you will be involved with people around the world. And whether you want to sell them something, buy something from them, or just talk—it helps if you speak their language.

● Because these days, it's common to travel around the world. The more languages you are familiar with, the easier it will be for you to get around, enjoy yourself, make new friends, and understand them, as well as have them understand you.

● Because English is made up of words from many languages, other languages share similar words, and textbooks, articles and even stories are often filled with foreign words and phrases. In other words, by learning a foreign language, your English will improve!

● Because foreign words and terms are actually very common in conversation and general reading materials, you won't be "lost" or "embarrassed" when you encounter them. You'll "speak the language."

● And, because it's lots of fun! You'll be proud of yourself. And you can expand on what you learn as much as you want to.

● Lastly, one day, you might be glad you can ask, "Where am I?" "How much is that?" "Which way to the bathroom?"—and understand the answer!

WHAT IS JAPANESE?

Japanese is the language of more than 100 million people who live on the 4 islands of Japan, as well as the island of Okinawa. Japanese is also widely used, especially at home, by immigrant families in Hawaii, the western coast of the United States, Brazil, and other parts of South America.

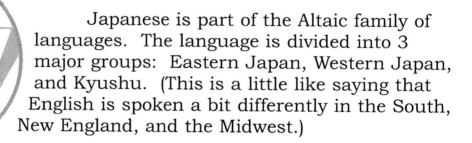

Japanese is part of the Altaic family of languages. The language is divided into 3 major groups: Eastern Japan, Western Japan, and Kyushu. (This is a little like saying that English is spoken a bit differently in the South, New England, and the Midwest.)

Like many other countries, Japan has "borrowed" many words from other cultures. This is especially true in modern times, when global communications, computers, business, and popular slang have made some words become more common in other languages. "Hamburger" is just one example!

While you are probably familiar with the beautiful Japanese *calligraphy* form of writing, we will not be using that in this book. In 1855, an American missionary created a way to write Japanese in the Roman letters we use in English. (Thank goodness!)

JAPAN

YOU KNOW JAPANESE ALREADY!

Have you ever used Fuji film in your camera? Ridden in a Mazda automobile? Eaten Sushi? Written a haiku poem? Zoomed off on a Kawasaki? Made a copy on a Samsung copier? Used a Conica camera or watched a Sony television? If so, you can see that you encounter Japanese words each day, especially in exported products such as cameras, film, cars, computers and electronics.

The study of U. S. history is filled with Japanese words, especially related to World War II. Banzai, Okinawa, Nagasaki, and Hiroshima are such words.

On a more pleasant note, perhaps you have seen the beautiful miniature *bonsai* plants, tasted *o-cha* (tea), sat on a *tatami* (mat), drank *Sake* (well, I hope not!), seen a *geisha* girl, sung *Karaoke*, used chopsticks, tried Judo, seen a Samurai warrior on an old movie, watched Sumo wrestling, worn a *kimono*, eaten *sukiyaki*, or said *sayonara*? If so, you know more Japanese than you thought you did!

It is not surprising that with the many Japanese tourists in America, Japanese Americans, Japanese corporations, and Japanese students, that we should fairly easily pick up their language. The Japanese certainly go to a lot of trouble to learn English. So now, it's your turn to learn a little Japanese!

HAVE YOU EVER SEEN JAPANESE KITES? THEY ARE VERY COLORFUL, BEAUTIFUL & SOMETIMES VERY LARGE. KITE FLYING IS A REAL ART IN JAPAN!

JAPANESE, IF YOU PLEASE!

I'll give you some information on Japan, and you do the same for me by answering the questions below!

1. Japan is an island country of Asia. Its 4 main islands are: Hokkaido, Honshu, Kyushu, and Shikoku. The word Japan most closely means:
- ◯ a) "Land of many islands"
- ◯ b) "Land of trees and flowers"
- ◯ c) "Land of the rising sun"

(The Japanese pronounce their country's name *Nihon* or *Nippon*.)

2. Japan was founded more than 2,000 years ago. The country (counting its islands and the water in between them) is about 2,000 miles long. Fuji-san is the highest and most beautiful
___ ___ ___ ___ ___ ___ ___ ___ in Japan. You often see pictures of it covered in snow. It is 12,387 feet high.

3. Japan's major religious groups are Buddhists, Shintoists, and
___ ___ ___ ___ ___ ___ ___ ___ ___ ___ ___.

4. In Japan, a person's family (what we would call "last" name) comes:
- ◯ a) before
- ◯ b) after their given (what we would call "first") name

JAPANESE PEOPLE!

1. Just like we have prejudice in our country, the Japanese have a group that they show prejudice against. These are the *burakumin*, or "outcasts." They often live in ghetto-like conditions. They may do menial jobs such as taking care of cemeteries or repairing *geta*, which are:

- a) radios
- b) foot-clogs
- c) bicycles

2. The largest city that the Japanese people live in is:

- a) Yokohama
- b) Osaka
- c) Tokyo

3. To buy things, Japanese people use money called:

- a) gen
- b) zen
- c) yen

4. The Ginza is Tokyo's main:

- a) shopping area
- b) government area
- c) cherry blossom area

5. *Giri* is the Japanese word for "doing the right thing" such as not cheating on a test. *Ninjo* means how you feel, emotionally, about someone, such as a girlfriend. Which word applies to stealing? To your mother?

MINDING YOUR MANNERS!

As you know, Americans do a lot of business with Japanese. Sometimes we don't seem to understand them, nor they us—and I don't just mean the language! Perhaps the following will help.

1. In America, we think being an individual is very important. In Japan, perhaps because they live so closely on their crowded islands, they think group harmony is more important. *Ningen*, their word for people, means:
- ◯ a) humans in relationship with others
- ◯ b) individuals working alone.

2. In Japan, *omote* is a formal situation, such as a wedding, where everything should be done very properly. *Ura* is an informal situation, when you can "let your hair down" a little more. So, if you are with your friends, you are in an _____ mode; and, if you are giving an oral report in front of the class, you are probably in an _____ mode!

3. The living generations in a Japanese household are called *ie*. They care for their ancestors by remembering them with offerings. In a Japanese household, the *ie* can include several families living together at the same time. The people in these families may or may not be related. Who are the *ie* in your home?

4. In America, we have Mother's Day and Father's Day and many other holidays. Japan has a

____ ____ ____ ____ ____ ____ ____ ____' ____ Day!

5. There are 2 kinds of marriage in Japan: *ren'ai* (for love) and *miai* (or arranged by others.) Which type of marriage do you think your older sister would prefer?!

FAMILY TIME!

1. *Katei* is the husband-wife unit in a family. Almost everyone in Japan gets married. Divorce is not very common in Japan. The mother plays a very important role in the Japanese family. She has the difficult job of making sure her children are well-loved, but also are strongly disciplined so they can do well in school. (Sounds like American mothers!) Sometimes a mother is called by the nickname *kyoiku mama*, which means:
- ○ a) mean mama
- ○ b) loving/strick mama
- ○ c) education mama

2. Some Japanese women work *pato* or part-time. This does not necessarily mean they work short hours, but that they are not full members of the company and so are not entitled to all the benefits that others may be. Women with more time may study *ikebana* which is:
- ○ a) the art of flower arranging
- ○ b) the study of English
- ○ c) Japanese cooking

3. Here are some words related to the Japanese home; can you match them?

WORD	MEANING
Ma	Wooden beam
Fusuma	Sliding door
Futon	Portable bed
Kitatsu	Fire hearth

FASHION & FOOD, JAPANESE-STYLÉ!

1. The traditional Japanese dress for a woman is the *kimono*. Today it is used primarily for special occasions. A *kimono* is an ankle-length wrap-around gown with long sleeves, tied with a wide sash. A *yukata* is a sleeping gown worn in an inn; to sleep in at home, you wear a *ryokan*. But most Japanese I see just wear *jipan*, or ___ ___ ___ ___ ___!

2. The main food in the Japanese diet is *gohan* or rice. Each meal is accompanied by *tsukemono* which are:
- ○ a) bread and butter
- ○ b) pickled vegetables
- ○ c) octopus or squid

3. *Miso* is Japanese:
- ○ a) meat
- ○ b) soup
- ○ c) desert

4. If my Mom bought some *panti sutokkingu,* what would she get? If my brother bought a *tatoru nekku*, what kind of a shirt would he get?

5. Make a guess at these Japanese colors!: *kuro* as night; pretty *ao* eyes; chocolate is *cha iro*; grass is *midori iro*; pumpkins are *orenji*; *pinku* is a girl baby color; *murasaki iro* is a royal color; like a *aka* rubber ball; a *shiro* wedding dress; *ki iro* flowers are always cheerful!

A GOOD JAPANESE SPORT!

As you may know, we really enjoy Japanese ping pong and volleyball and they love baseball and golf. See if you can match the Japanese term on the left with what it means on the right. Since this is about sports, you'll receive 1 point for each correct answer!

JAPANESE TERM	MEANING
_____ 1. Kyudo	A. A form of chess
_____ 2. Sumo	B. Arts
_____ 3. Martial	C. Archery
_____ 4. Heya	D. Means "empty hand"
_____ 5. Karate	E. Wrestling
_____ 6. Shogi	F. Domino-type board game
_____ 7. Mah-jongg	G. Wrestling Studio
_____ 8. Pachinko	H. Pinball

What is your favorite Japanese sport? American sport? Are they one and the same?

A TRIP TO JAPAN!

While we know the Japanese love to travel, we like to be tourists too. So, let's go to their country:

1. In Japan, you can stay in a *ryokan*, or traditional Japanese
___ ___ ___.

2. You might sleep on a *futon* or floor pallet, which is put down on top of *tatami* or rice straw matting. This takes the place of an American ___ ___ ___.

3. To get from one place to another, you may ride a high-speed "bullet" ___ ___ ___ ___ ___!

4. Everyone enjoys a visit to a Japanese religious shrine or temple where you might see a statue of ___ ___ ___ ___ ___ ___.

5. Sapporo, which has a Snow Festival is a good place to go to ___ ___ ___.

6. Perhaps a student will invite you to visit their *kazoku* or
___ ___ ___ ___ ___ ___ at home.

7. You can get some pen and paper and try Japanese writing or ___ ___ ___ ___ ___ ___ ___ ___ ___ ___.

8. What are those men doing with those gardens?
They are practicing the art of *bonsai*, or growing very small ___ ___ ___ ___ ___.

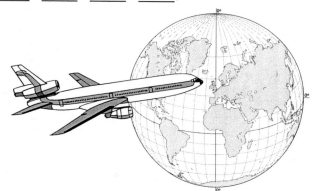

FUJI FUN!

1. Mt. Fuji is a __ __ __ __ __ __ __!
Many of Japan's crops are grown in *ando*, which means "dark soil."
Where does *ando* come from?

2. ___ ___ ___ ___ is harvested in paddies.

3. It is very entertaining to visit a Kabuki theater, where traditional Japanese ___ ___ ___ ___ ___ ___ are performed.

4. The *Diet* is the building where the Japanese:
○ a) government assembles
○ b) weight watchers meet
○ c) chefs cook traditional foods

5. The Japanese *cha-no-yu*, or ___ ___ ___ ceremony is a very special event. It can be performed by a *geisha*, which is a professional hostess trained in song, dance, poetry and conversation.

6. If I wanted to buy electronic products in Japan, I would ask for the following and get what?: (Go ahead, take a good guess!)

kasetto pureya _____

pasonaru konputa _____

denshi gamu _____

terebi _____

bideo rekoda _____

JAPANESE HISTORY!

The *Kojiki* or Record of Ancient Matters and the *Nihon-shoki* or Chronicles of Japan tell the ancient history of this island nation. Japanese history is divided into *jidai* or periods. Japanese history can also be divided into the following categories: *genshi* (early); *kodai* (ancient); *chusei* (medieval); *kinsei* (early modern); and *kindai* (modern.)

Researchers learned a lot about Japanese history from Jomon, an early form of Japanese pottery, *doboko* (weapons), and *dotaku* (bells.) Like the American Indian, early Japanese buried their dead in *kofun* or burial mounds. *Haniwa*, or grave figures, made of clay represented dead family members.

Early Japanese mythological gods had interesting names such as Isanami and Izanagi (male and female), Amaterasu Omikami, the sun goddess, and her brother Susano-o-no-Mikoto, the storm god. Early peoples were organized into clans or *uji*. Early Japanese believed in spirits or *kami*.

Later, an elite military class came about; they were called the *samurai*. Their leader became known as the *shogun*. These warriors would sometimes kill themselves by *seppuku*, by cutting out their own guts with a knife. This was considered an honorable way to die!

History makes me hungry! If you stop by a Japanese kiosk and ask for the following, what do you think you will get?: *kyandi*; *chuin gamu*; *chokoreto*; *kukki*. (Think about it! Listen carefully to the words. I'll bet you guess them all correctly!)

REMEMBER PEARL HARBOR!

Although we are friends and trading partners with the country of Japan now, there was a time when Japan was the enemy of the United States. This began in 1941 when Japan bombed the American military base at Pearl Harbor on the island of Oahu in Hawaii.

Kamikaze is Japanese for "divine wind." During World War II, *Kamikaze* pilots willingly sacrificed their lives if it meant they could destroy enemy aircraft in the process.

Later, Americans would come to know the names of the Japanese cities of *Hiroshima* and *Nagasaki*, where the United States dropped atomic bombs to try and put an end to the war.

INTERVIEW ACTIVITY:

Here's your chance to do some important oral history. Find out who, if anyone, in your family remembers about World War II. If they are old enough, they might even have fought in this war. Find out how they felt about the war then, and how they feel about the war now. Why was this war fought? Who won? Who lost? How was history changed? Did we learn anything from this war? What? Add other questions you would like to have answered. If you get a chance, ask a Japanese person what they think about these questions. Take notes; maybe even video the people you interview. Save all this—one day you will be glad you did!

JAPAN PLACES!

Here are some Japanese terms, places, etc. that you should know:

The Sea of Japan is called *Nihon-kai* in Japanese.

A *tsunami* is the Japanese word for tidal wave.

Japan Clover is a pink or purple flower native to Asia that grows in America.

The Japan Current is a warm ocean current in the Pacific Ocean. The Japanese call the current *Kuroshio*.

The Japan Trench is a long, narrow depression in the floor of the Pacific Ocean. Such areas are often sites of earthquake activity. Deep ocean trenches are also where many strange sea creatures live without light!

The Japanese Beetle is an insect native to Japan that was accidentally introduced into the United States. A garden pest, it eats the leaves of fruit trees, doing around $100 million in damage each year.

A Japanese Spaniel is a toy spaniel raised as a pet. It is also called the *Chin-Chin*. It looks similar to the Pekingese.

Japanning is a process where several coats of varnish are painted onto decorative objects such as furniture to make a hard, shiny surface.

JAPAN

CHOPSTICK TIME!

Japanese food is very popular in America. See if you can substitute the Japanese word in each sentence from the list below!

WORD BANK

NORI	WASABI	TOFU	DAIKON	SHUNGIKU
SHOYU	SERI	SHITAKE	TEMPURA	SUSHI

1. The ___ ___ ___ ___ ___ ___ or giant white radish would be good in a salad.

2. ___ ___ ___ ___ ___ or soybean sauce is commonly used in Japanese cooking.

3. ___ ___ ___ ___, or soybean curd, looks like vanilla custard.

4. Watch out for the ___ ___ ___ ___ ___ ___ or Japanese horseradish!

5. ___ ___ ___ ___ is Japanese parsley.

6. I didn't know you could eat ___ ___ ___ ___ ___ ___ ___ ___, or chrysanthemum leaves.

7. The ___ ___ ___ ___ ___ ___ ___ mushroom is very popular in fancy American restaurants.

8. ___ ___ ___ ___ is one kind of seaweed used in Japanese soups.

9. Seafood eaten raw is called ___ ___ ___ ___ ___.

10. A light batter covers shrimp cooked ___ ___ ___ ___ ___ ___ ___ style.

IN CASE OF AN EMERGENCY DO YOU DIAL HONORABLE 911?

ALERT!

Who knows when you might need some Japanese words to "HELP!" you? Try these when you need them; I don't think you'll need any help to figure them out!

1. If you yell, "*tasukete*!" that means you need ____ ____ ____ ____.

2. *Keisatsu o yonde dudasai* means "Call the
____ ____ ____ ____ ____ ____."

3. Holler "*KAJI!*" loudly to tell others that there is a
____ ____ ____ ____.

4. If someone is in an accident you ask a Japanese bystander to *isha o yonde kudasai,* or "Get a
____ ____ ____ ____ ____ ____."

5. If you need a doctor, you might say, "*byoki desu,*" or
"I'm ____ ____ ____."

6. "*Michi ni mayoi mashita*" is a common complaint among tourists who take a wrong turn. It means ____'____
____ ____ ____ ____.

7. If someone is bothering you, you might advise them *hitori ni shite oite kudasai,* or, "____ ____ ____ ____ ____ ____
____ ____ ____ ____ ____!

8. If someone snatches your purse, scream: "*dorobo o tsuka maete kudasai!*" which means "Stop ____ ____ ____ ____ ____!"

GETTING TO KNOW YOU!

Whether you visit Japan or meet someone from Japan in your own country, it's always nice to be able to converse a little bit. Sometimes, it's essential, as you'll see in question 8 below!

QUESTION	ANSWER	MEANS
1. How do you greet someone each A.M.?	ohayo gozaimasu	_ _ _ _ _ _ _ _ _ _ _ _
2. What do you say when you make a mistake?	sumimasen	_ _ _ _ _ _ _ _
3. What word should follow any request?	o-negai shimashu	_ _ _ _ _ _
4. If someone pays you a compliment, what do you say?	arigato	_ _ _ _ _ _ _ _ _
5. Do you want a million dollars?	hai!	_ _ _
6. Do you want to catch a cold?	iie	_ _
7. What are you asking?	eigo o hana-shimasu	Do you speak _ _ _ _ _ _ _ _?
8. What's the most important question?	o-tearai wa doko desu ka	Where is the _ _ _ _ _ _ _ _ _?

Eigo o hana-shimasu?

THIS MYSTERIOUS LANGUAGE!

Where does Japanese come from? No one really knows. Japan, its people, customs, and language were almost totally isolated for more than 2,000 years. This produced a very unique language like no other on earth!

However, many foreign words (to them!) have been adopted into the Japanese language. Some of these include:

DISCO   COCOA   MONORAIL   MANAGER   GOLF

Write a sentence with each of the words above, in the way a Japanese girl living in Tokyo might use them:

1. _____

2. _____

3. _____

4. _____

5. _____

OPPOSITES ATTRACT!

It's true! See if you can memorize some of these Japanese opposites:

ENGLISH	JAPANESE
big/small	okii/chisai
fast/slow	hayai/osoi
hot/cold	atsui/samui
full/empty	ippai/kara
easy/hard	yasashi/muzukashii
heavy/light	omoi/karui
open/shut	aiteiru/shimatteiru
right/wrong	tadashii/machigai
old/new	furui/atarashii
old/young	toshitotteiru/wakai
beautiful/ugly	utsukushii/minkui
good/bad	yoi/warui
better/worse	yori yori/yori warui
early/late	hayai/osoi
cheap/expensive	yasui/takai
near/far	chkai/toi
here/there	koko/asoko
a little/a lot	sukoshi/takusan
more/less	motto oku/motto sukunaku

USEFUL WORDS!

寿
Happiness

You never know when these everyday Japanese words will come in handy! See if you can figure out the word from the sentence.

1. Let's jump *no ue* the trampoline!

2. Let's go *e* the mall!

3. You can have dessert *no ato* you eat your Japanese veggies.

4. Alice went *o toshite* the looking glass.

5. There will be no intermission *no aida* the movie.

6. Nothing will ever come *no aida* us.

7. The center of the earth is *shita ni* my feet.

8. The sun is *no maue ni* my head.

9. In case of an earthquake, crawl *no shita ni* your desk!

10. The *no naka ni* of Mt. Fuji is filled with lava.

11. To climb stairs, you have to go *ue*.

12. You are my one and *dake* friend!

Gohan is Japanese rice.
Yen is Japanese money.
A *samurai* is a warrior.

YUMMY JAPANESE FOOD!

From the menu of delicious dishes below, select several that you have tasted, or would like to try!

OUR MENU TODAY!

Kushiage	Chicken, pork or seafood + vegetables on a skewer, deep fried
Oden	Fish stew with seaweed; often served by *yatai* or street vendors
Okonomiyaki	Japanese pancake with shrimp + veggies
Shabu-Shabu	Thin-sliced beef with vegetables
Soba	Noodle dish; if you're still hungry, have *omori,* or seconds!
Sukiyaki	Thick beef + vegetables cooked over an open fire
Sushi	Rice with raw fish & vegetables
Tempura	Seafood & veggies coated in an egg/flour batter & deep fried
Unagi	Grilled eel
Yakitori	Barbecued chicken on a skewer
Yosenabe	Chicken soup in a pot or *nabe*

CHOP-CHOP WITH CHOPSTICKS!

Chopsticks were introduced to Japan from China in the 5th century. To use chopsticks, hold the upper stick between your thumb and first two fingers. Keep the lower stick still with your second and third fingers. Hold the sticks with 1/3 above your hands and 2/3 below. In a restaurant, you'll be brought half-split wooden chopsticks, which you can easily pull apart to use. These are discarded after the meal. However, in a Japanese home, re-usable chopsticks of various materials are used. ("It's your turn to wash the chopsticks. No, I did it last night!")

Chopstick Tip: If you are served soup, with no spoon, but only chopsticks, what do you do? Use your chopsticks to get any food out of the soup, then drink the broth right from the bowl—it's ok to make slurpy noises!

Places to eat in Japan include:
- *kissaten*, or coffee shop
- *nomiya*, or sake bar
- *resutoran*, regular Japanese or American-style restaurant
- *ryoriya*, Japanese restaurant where you can dine in an
- *ozashiki* or private room
- *koryori-ha*, or small Japanese eatery
- *robatayaki*, or country-style restaurant where food is cooked on a *ro*, or inset hearth in front of the guests
- *sunakku ba*, or snack bar!
- *yatai*, or street stalls or push carts; they serve roasted sweet potatoes, noodles, soup, stew or barbecued food

If someone offers you an *oshibori*, don't eat it—it's a hot or cold towel with which to wash your hands and face!

Lunch is *chushoku*; dinner is *yushoku*.

THE RIGHT DIRECTION!

See if you can match the direction with its Japanese word!:

_____ 1. North   A. Minami
_____ 2. South   B. Higashi
_____ 3. East   C. Nishi
_____ 4. West   D. Kita

Going Bye-Bye In Japan!
Don't these sound like fun places to go, in any language?

ENGLISH	JAPANESE
aquarium	suizokukan
art gallery	garo
castle	shiro
cave	dokutsu
fair	hakurankai
flea market	nomi no ichi
fort	josai
fountain	funsui
gardens	teien
harbor	minato
kabuki theater	kabukiza
library	toshokan
market	soin
museum	hakubutsukan
observatory	tenmondai
palace	kyuden
park	koen
Olympic stadium	orinpikku kyogijo
zoo	dobutsuen

LET'S TAKE A JAPANESE GARDEN TOUR!

From the list of English words below, see if you can find their Japanese counterpart in the tour below!

WORD BANK

BRIDGE	FARM	FOREST	GARDEN	HILL
HOUSE	ISLAND	LAKE	MOUNTAIN	FOOTPATH
ROAD	VALLEY	VILLAGE	WATERFALL	CHERRY TREE

TOUR-A-LURA-LURA!

Our class went on a tour of a Japanese *niwa*. In many ways, it seemed like a scavenger hunt! it was a lot of fun and we got a lot more exercise than I expected!

First we took a small *komichi* to the garden. It lead us past a snow-covered *yama*. We saw crops and animals on a small *nojo*. It was very cool when we passed through a *mori* of large trees.

In the garden there was a beautiful *sakura*; the petals were just beginning to fall on the ground. We all enjoyed walking over the *hashi* to get to the other side of the *mizuumi* in the garden.

When we left the *niwa*, we took a *michi* which took us over an *oka* where we saw a small *mura* in a broad and fertile *tani* where they were growing tea. In the middle of another *mizuumi*, we saw a *shima* with a pretty, Japanese-style *ie* on it.

Best of all, we got to walk beneath a flowing *taki* on the way back home!

KABUKI TO YOU TOO!

The Japanese theater is famous around the world. They have 3 kinds of traditional theater which are unique:

Noh: This is the oldest of the Japanese stage arts. It dates back to the 13th century. Men, wearing colorful, stiff costumes and wooden masks perform in slow motion. The only scenery is a backdrop of painted pine trees. The stage is open on 3 sides.

Kabuki: Begun in the 16th century. There is a very large stage, fancy sets and costumes, and lots of fast action! All the actors are men; the ones who play the female roles have practiced since early childhood! Shows may last 4 hours, but you can buy tickets to just part of a show.

Bunraku: This is the famous Japanese puppet theater. The puppet dolls are 3-4 & 1/2 feet high. It takes a master puppeteer & 2 assistants to operate each doll. The puppeteers wear all black outfits while they do their work. The dolls move on a waist-high platform on a stage.

GEISHA GIRLS!

Geisha are trained hostesses. Since early childhood they have practiced singing, dancing & playing the shamisen, a Japanese musical instrument. They pour sake (rice wine) for guests. Their main job is to be pleasant and entertaining, to help "break the ice" among guests, and to keep the conversation going. (Sounds like a geisha would be handy on a first date!)

A GOOD SPORT!

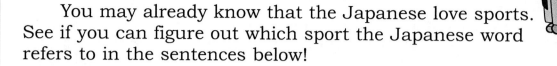

You may already know that the Japanese love sports. See if you can figure out which sport the Japanese word refers to in the sentences below!

1. A *sumo* match between 2 ___ ___ ___ ___ ___ ___ ___ ___ ___ who each weigh 200-350 pounds is a big event!

2. Even in America, we now have *judo*, *kendo* and ___ ___ ___ ___ ___ ___.

3. The sport of *yakyu* is as popular in Japan as it is in America, hot dogs and peanuts too!

4. The sport of *basukett boru* will really put you through your hoops!

5. *Sakka*, in any language, is the most popular sport around the world.

6. When it snows on the mountains, *suki* is popular.

7. If you like to do laps, *suiei* may be for you!

8. The Japanese "love" *tenisu*.

9. The sport of *bareboru* will net you a good time!

10. I'll bet you'd like to go to the track and see some *keiba*.

11. Better wear your "gloves" if you go *bokushingu*!

12. Do you wear *ragubi* shirts to play *ragubi*?

PAGE 8: 1-c; 2-mountain; 3-Christians; 4-a

PAGE 9: 1-b; 2-c; 3-c; 4-a; 5-Giri; Ninjo

PAGE 10: 1-a; 2-ura, onote; 4-Children's

PAGE 11: 1-c; 2-a; 3-the definition beside each word is correct!

PAGE 12: 1-jeans; 2-b; 3-b; 4-pantyhose, turtleneck; 5-black, blue, brown, green, orange, pink, purple, red, white, yellow

PAGE 13: 1-c; 2-E; 3-B; 4-G; 5-D; 6-A; 7-F; 8-H

PAGE 14: 1-inn; 2-bed; 3-train; 4-Buddha; 5-ski; 6-family; 7-calligraphy; 8-trees

PAGE 15: 1-volcano; 2-rice; 3-dances; 4-a; 5-tea; 6-music cassette, personal computer, electronic game, television, video recorder

PAGE 19: 1-daikon; 2-shoyu; 3-tofu; 4-wasabi; 5-seri; 6-shungiku;-7-shitake; 8-nori; 9-sushi; 10-tempura

PAGE 20: 1-Help; 2-police; 3-fire; 4-doctor; 5-ill; 6-I'm lost; 7-Leave me alone; 8-thief

PAGE 21: 1-good morning; 2-excuse me; 3-please; 4-thank you; 5-yes; 6-no; 7-English; 8-bathroom

PAGE 24: 1-on; 2-to; 3-after; 4-through; 5-during; 6-between; 7-beneath; 8-above; 9-under; 10-inside; 11-up; 12-only

PAGE 25: 1-on; 2-to; 3-after; 4-through; 5-during; 6-between; 7-below; 8-above; 9-under; 10-inside; 11-up; 12-only

PAGE 27: 1-D; 2-A; 3-B; 4-C

PAGE 28: garden, footpath, mountain, farm, forest, cherry tree, bridge, lake; garden, road, hill, village, valley, lake, island, house, waterfall

PAGE 30: 1-wrestlers; 2-karate; 3-baseball; 4-basketball; 5-soccer; 6-skiing; 7-swimming; 8-tennis; 9-volleyball; 10-horse racing; 11-boxing; 12-rugby

CERTIFICATE OF ACHIEVEMENT

This Certificate of Achievement is to bear witness that

Name: _____

officially completed this book and can speak Japanese.

Signed: _____ Dr. G.E. Nius _____   Date: _____